WHAT I KNOW ABOUT

GRATITUDE

Gibbs Smith

First Edition
29 28 27 26 25 5 4 3 2 1

Published by
Gibbs Smith
570 N. Sportsplex Dr.
Kaysville, Utah 84037

1.800.835.4993 orders
www.gibbs-smith.com

Designed by Sheryl Dickert
Printed and bound in China
This product is made of FSC®-certified and other controlled material.

MIX
Paper | Supporting responsible forestry
FSC® C208677
FSC www.fsc.org

Library of Congress Control Number: 2024951223
ISBN: 978-1-4236-6862-6

INTRODUCTION

Living a life of gratitude makes you happy. Neuroscientists have shown that feeling and expressing thanks increases feelings of satisfaction and well-being. It leads to better relationships at home and at work, boosts mental health, and creates a better, richer, more joyful life.

What I Know About Gratitude brings together 125 quotations celebrating giving thanks.

In this volume, you'll find quotes from actors, writers, religious leaders, athletes, philosophers, and others who share insights and inspiration about being grateful. Thomas Merton, Brené Brown, Eckhart Tolle, Cicero, and the Dalai Lama are among the many luminaries included here.

This little book is filled with joyful reminders about the power of being grateful.

Piglet noticed that even though he had a Very Small Heart, it could hold a rather large amount of

GRATITUDE.

—A. A. MILNE

Happiness cannot be traveled to, owned, earned, worn, or consumed. Happiness is the spiritual experience of living every minute with love, grace, and gratitude.

—DENIS WAITLEY

Acknowledging the good that you already have in your life is the foundation for all abundance.

—ECKHART TOLLE

As we express our gratitude,
we must never forget that the
highest appreciation is not to utter
words, but to live by them.

—JOHN F. KENNEDY

Gratitude is riches. Complaint is poverty.

—DORIS DAY

Feeling gratitude and not expressing it is like wrapping a present and not giving it.

—WILLIAM ARTHUR WARD

Being grateful does not mean that everything is necessarily good. It just means that you can accept it as a gift.

—ROY T. BENNETT

It's up to us to choose contentment and thankfulness now—and to stop imagining that we have to have everything perfect before we'll be happy.

—JOANNA GAINES

Living in a state of gratitude is the gateway to grace.

—ARIANNA HUFFINGTON

Gratitude is the closest thing to beauty manifested in an emotion.

—MINDY KALING

The only thing you should feel entitled to is gratitude.

—J. S. MASON

Gratitude is the power to connect with the cosmos and harness its energy.

—SUKANT RATNAKAR

GRATITUDE IS A POSTURE OF YOUR HEART.

I believe that it has been a gatekeeper in my life and has brought on so many blessings.

—AMANDA KLOOTS

Gratitude helps you to grow and expand; gratitude brings joy and laughter into your life and into the lives of all those around you.

—EILEEN CADDY

Let us be grateful to the people who make us happy; they are the charming gardeners who make our souls blossom.

—MARCEL PROUST

Be mindful.

Be grateful.

Be positive.

Be true.

Be kind.

—ROY T. BENNETT

Walk as if you are kissing the earth with your feet.

—THICH NHAT HANH

True wisdom cannot be obtained
unless it is built on a foundation
of true humility and gratitude.

—GORDON B. HINCKLEY

We can complain

because rose

bushes have thorns,

or rejoice because

thorns have roses.

—JEAN-BAPTISTE ALPHONSE KARR

True happiness is to enjoy the present, without anxious dependence upon the future, not to amuse ourselves with either hopes or fears but to rest satisfied with what we have.

—SENECA

Cultivate the habit of being grateful for every good thing that comes to you, and to give thanks continuously. And because all things have contributed to your advancement, you should include all things in your gratitude.

—RALPH WALDO EMERSON

Let gratitude be the pillow upon which you kneel to say your nightly prayer.

—MAYA ANGELOU

If having a soul means being able to feel love and loyalty and gratitude, then animals are better off than a lot of humans.

—JAMES HERRIOT

Gratitude

is not only the greatest of virtues,

but the parent of all others.

—CICERO

Appreciation is a wonderful thing. It makes what is excellent in others belong to us as well.

—VOLTAIRE

It’s a funny thing about life, once you begin to take note of the things you are grateful for, you begin to lose sight of the things that you lack.

—GERMANY KENT

THE HIGHEST TRIBUTE TO THE DEAD IS NOT GRIEF BUT GRATITUDE.

—THORNTON WILDER

In normal life we hardly realize how much more we receive than we give, and life cannot be rich without such gratitude. It is so easy to overestimate the importance of our own achievements compared with what we owe to the help of others.

—DIETRICH BONHOEFFER

What separates privilege from entitlement is gratitude.

—BRENÉ BROWN

Not what we say about our blessings,

but how we use them, is the true

measure of our thanksgiving.

—W. T. PURKISER

If you want to find happiness,

find gratitude.

—STEVE MARABOLI

Gratitude is the ability to experience life as a gift.

—JOHN ORTBERG

The most beautiful moments in life are moments when you are expressing your joy, not when you are seeking it.

—JAGGI VASUDEV

An attitude of gratitude brings great things.

—YOGI BHAJAN

He who does not reflect his life back to God in gratitude does not know himself.

—ALBERT SCHWEITZER

I may not be where I want to be but I'm

thankful for not being where I used to be.

—HABEEB AKANDE

Gratitude bestows reverence . . .

. . . changing forever how we

experience life and the world.

—JOHN MILTON

When I started counting my blessings, my whole life turned around.

—WILLIE NELSON

WE OFTEN TAKE FOR GRANTED THE VERY THINGS THAT MOST DESERVE OUR GRATITUDE.

—CYNTHIA OZICK

Gratitude is when

memory is stored in the heart

and not in the mind.

—LIONEL HAMPTON

No duty is more urgent than that of returning thanks.

—JAMES ALLEN

Gratitude unlocks the fullness of life.

—MELODY BEATTIE

I am happy because I'm grateful.

I CHOOSE TO BE GRATEFUL.

That gratitude allows me to be

HAPPY.

—WILL ARNETT

Live a life full of humility,

gratitude, intellectual curiosity,

and never stop learning.

—GZA

When we focus on our gratitude, the tide of disappointment goes out and the tide of love rushes in.

—KRISTIN ARMSTRONG

The power of finding beauty
in the humblest things makes
home happy and life lovely.

—LOUISA MAY ALCOTT

Gratitude is the fairest

blossom which springs

from the soul.

—HENRY WARD BEECHER

When you arise in the morning give thanks for the food and for the joy of living. If you see no reason for giving thanks, the fault lies only in yourself.

—TECUMSEH

When eating fruit, remember

the one who planted the tree.

—VIETNAMESE PROVERB

I live by two words:

TENACITY

and

GRATITUDE.

—HENRY WINKLER

Gratitude is a divine emotion:

it fills the heart, but not to bursting;

it warms it, but not to fever.

—CHARLOTTE BRONTË

The heart that gives thanks
is a happy one, for we cannot
feel thankful and unhappy
at the same time.

—DOUGLAS WOOD

We would worry less if we praised more. Thanksgiving is the enemy of discontent and dissatisfaction.

—H. A. IRONSIDE

Wear gratitude like a cloak,

and it will feed every

corner of your life.

—RUMI

THOSE WHO ARE NOT GRATEFUL SOON BEGIN TO COMPLAIN OF EVERYTHING.

—THOMAS MERTON

Gratitude isn't a burdening emotion.

—LORETTA YOUNG

Never let the things you want make you forget the things you have.

—SANCHITA PANDEY

Gratitude is an antidote to negative emotions, a neutralizer of envy, hostility, worry, and irritation. It is savoring; it is not taking things for granted; it is present-oriented.

—SONJA LYUBOMIRSKY

GRATITUDE is the most exquisite form of courtesy.

—JACQUES MARITAIN

The more you practice the art of thankfulness,

the more you have to be thankful for.

—NORMAN VINCENT PEALE

Even if you don't have all the things you want, be grateful for the things you don't have that you don't want.

—BOB DYLAN

I am grateful for what I am and have.

My thanksgiving is perpetual.

—HENRY DAVID THOREAU

Take one thing with another, and the world is a pretty good sort of a world, and 'tis our duty to make the best of it and be

THANKFUL.

—BENJAMIN FRANKLIN

Fill the earth with your songs of gratitude.

—CHARLES SPURGEON

“THANK YOU”

is the best prayer that anyone could say.

—ALICE WALKER

I would maintain that thanks are the highest form of thought; and that gratitude is happiness doubled by wonder.

—G. K. CHESTERTON

There is no better excess in the world than the excess of gratitude.

—JEAN DE LA BRUYÈRE

He is a wise man who does not grieve for the things which he has not, but rejoices for those which he has.

—EPICTETUS

If the only prayer you said was

THANK YOU,

that would be enough.

—MEISTER ECKHART

When it comes to life the critical thing is whether you take things for granted or take them with gratitude.

—G. K. CHESTERTON

The soul that gives thanks can find comfort in everything; the soul that complains can find comfort in nothing.

—HANNAH WHITALL SMITH

The world has plenty and the promise of a new sunrise and sunset every day. What the world needs more of is people to appreciate and enjoy it.

—MICHAEL JOSEPHSON

SILENT GRATITUDE ISN'T MUCH USE TO ANYONE.

—GERTRUDE STEIN

Do not spoil what you have by desiring what you have not; remember that what you now have was once among the things you only hoped for.

—EPICURUS

When brimming with gratitude, one's heartbeat must surely result in outgoing love, the finest emotion we can ever know.

—BILL WILSON

Every once in a while, God allows you to stub your toe as a kind reminder to be grateful for the miraculous body attached to it.

—RICHELLE E. GOODRICH

The unthankful heart discovers no mercies; but the thankful heart will find, in every hour, some heavenly blessings.

—HENRY WARD BEECHER

Gratitude is a powerful catalyst for happiness. It's the spark that lights a fire of joy in your soul.

—AMY COLLETTE

When a person doesn't have gratitude, something is missing in his or her humanity. A person can almost be defined by his or her attitude to gratitude.

—ELIE WIESEL

The best way to show my gratitude is to accept everything, even my problems, with joy.

—MOTHER TERESA

Gratitude can transform common days into thanksgivings, turn routine jobs into joy, and change ordinary opportunities into blessings.

—WILLIAM ARTHUR WARD

Appreciation can make a day, even change a life.

Your willingness to put it into words is all that is necessary.

—MARGARET COUSINS

Gratitude—warm, sincere, intense, when it takes possession of the bosom—fills the soul to overflowing and scarce leaves room for any other sentiment or thought.

—JOHN QUINCY ADAMS

Be thankful for what you have; you'll end up having more. If you concentrate on what you don't have, you will never, ever have enough.

—OPRAH WINFREY

Gratitude is the

sign of noble souls.

—AESOP

The discipline of gratitude is the explicit effort to acknowledge that all I am and have is given to me as a gift of love, a gift to be celebrated with joy.

—HENRI NOUWEN

We are constituted so that simple acts of kindness, such as giving to charity or expressing gratitude, have a positive effect on our long-term moods.

—PAUL BLOOM

Always have an attitude of gratitude.

—STERLING K. BROWN

Inner contentment doesn’t come from having all we want; but rather from wanting and appreciating and being grateful for all we have.

—DALAI LAMA

Be grateful for what you have

and stop complaining—

it bores everybody else,

does you no good, and

doesn't solve any problems.

—ZIG ZIGLAR

Happiness is itself a kind of gratitude.

—JOSEPH WOOD KRUTCH

Have gratitude for all that you have,

and you can be happy exactly as you are.

—MANDY INGBER

When you know in your bones that your body is a sacred gift, you move in the world with an effortless grace. Gratitude and humility rise up spontaneously.

—DEBBIE FORD

I believe gratitude leads to happiness.

—NAFESSA WILLIAMS

The thankful receiver bears a plentiful harvest.

—WILLIAM BLAKE

To give thanks in solitude is enough. Thanksgiving has wings and goes where it must go. Your prayer knows much more about it than you do.

—VICTOR HUGO

If a fellow isn't thankful for what he's got, he isn't likely to be thankful for what he's going to get.

—FRANK A. CLARK

Gratitude is what we radiate when we experience grace, and the soul was made to run on grace the way a 747 runs on rocket fuel.

—JOHN ORTBERG

Joy is the simplest form of gratitude.

—POPE JOHN PAUL II

It's wonderful to be grateful. To have that gratitude well out from deep within you and pour out in waves. Once you truly experience this, you will never want to give it up.

—SRIKUMAR RAO

At times, our own light goes out and is rekindled by a spark from another person. Each of us has cause to think with deep gratitude of those who have lighted the flame within us.

—ALBERT SCHWEITZER

Gratitude turns what we have into enough.

—ANONYMOUS

Thankfulness is the beginning of gratitude.

Gratitude is the completion of thankfulness.

Thankfulness may consist merely of words.

Gratitude is shown in acts.

—HENRI-FRÉDÉRIC AMIEL

Gratitude will shift you to a higher frequency and you will attract much better things.

—RHONDA BYRNE

There are two kinds of gratitude:

The sudden kind we feel for what we take; the larger kind we feel for what we give.

—EDWIN ARLINGTON ROBINSON

THE MORE GRATEFUL I AM, THE MORE BEAUTY I SEE.

—MARY DAVIS

The deepest craving of human nature is the need to be appreciated.

—WILLIAM JAMES

There is a calmness to a life lived in gratitude, a quiet joy.

—RALPH H. BLUM

It’s so much easier to learn to love
what you have instead of yearning
always for what you’re missing,
or what you imagine you’re missing.
It’s so much more peaceful.

—ANNA QUINDLEN

The root of joy is gratefulness.

—DAVID STEINDL-RAST

We can only be said to be alive in those moments when our hearts are conscious of our treasures.

—THORNTON WILDER

Being thankful is not always experienced as a natural state of existence; we must work at it, akin to a type of strength training for the heart.

—LARISSA GOMEZ

If you concentrate on finding

whatever is good in every situation,

you will discover that your life will

suddenly be filled with gratitude,

a feeling that nurtures the soul.

—RABBI HAROLD KUSHNER

Gratitude for the present moment and the fullness of life now is the true prosperity.

—ECKHART TOLLE

Be grateful to those who have helped you along the way.

—MARTIN LUTHER KING, JR.

NOTHING IS MORE HONORABLE THAN A GRATEFUL HEART.

—SENECA

When you are grateful, fear disappears and abundance appears.

—ANTHONY ROBBINS

GRATITUDE IS
THE MEMORY OF
THE HEART.

—JEAN-BAPTISTE MASSIEU

Every minute of every hour of every day you are making the world, just as you are making yourself, and you might as well do it with generosity and kindness and style.

—REBECCA SOLNIT

Saying thank you is more than good manners. It is good spirituality.

—ALFRED PAINTER

Gratitude turns what we have

into enough, and more.

It turns denial into acceptance,

chaos to order,

confusion to clarity.

—MELODY BEATTIE

Gratitude is always in one's power.

—ABIGAIL ADAMS

Gratitude is a currency that we can mint for ourselves and spend without fear of bankruptcy.

—FRED DE WITT VAN AMBURGH

Gratitude and love are not to be had

for the asking; they are not to be bought. . . .

What we should seek,

rather than gratitude or love,

is the respect of the world.

—ELEANOR ROOSEVELT

The roots of all goodness lie in the soil of appreciation for goodness.

—DALAI LAMA